CW01638415

Unbelievable Lawsuit Stories

The 100 Funniest, Weirdest & Craziest Lawsuits in History

Thomas Maddison

Copyright © 2025 by Thomas Maddison

All rights reserved.

No part of this book may be reproduced in any form or by any electronic or mechanical means, including information storage and retrieval systems, without written permission from the author, except for the use of brief quotations in a book review.

eBook ISBN: 978-1-916815-46-9

Print ISBN: 978-1-916815-47-6

Typeface: Crimson Pro

Book cover elements from Creative Fabrica: License #87652775

Contents

Introduction

Introduction

Before we get to the juicy stories, let's get a quick introduction out of the way.

I'm Thomas, a 52-year-old attorney from Boston, MA. For the past three decades, I've spent more time in courtrooms and legal libraries than I care to admit. I've seen my fair share of lawsuits—some justified, some questionable, and some so downright bizarre that I had to double-check the paperwork to make sure I wasn't being pranked.

That's what led me to write this book. I've always had a love for research and a fascination with the strange, unexpected corners of the legal world. Most people think of lawsuits as dry, complicated, and—let's be honest—boring. But if you dig a little deeper, you'll find that the legal system is home to some of the most ridiculous, hilarious, and mind-boggling cases you can imagine. I'm talking about the kind of lawsuits that make you stop and say, Wait... someone actually sued over that?

Like the Australian teen who sued subway for having sandwiches that were too short. Or the woman who took a TV channel to court because of getting a weather forecast wrong. And let's not forget the classic case of the kidnapper that tried to sue his hostages.

Some of these cases make you laugh, some make you shake your head in disbelief, and others make you wonder how on earth they ever made it past the courthouse steps. But one thing's for sure—every single one of them is a wild ride.

I've broken the book into five chapters, each focusing on a different category of crazy lawsuits. We've got:

1 The Clashes of Corporate Giants – *Corporate lawyers getting a little excitable!*

2 Taking on the Corporate World – *When Joe Public bravely took on the big dogs!*

3 When Companies Get Angry – *Companies getting their own book on the little man (and woman).*

4 Most Unusual Lawsuits – *Some of these are quite simply just ridiculous.*

5 Historic Lawsuits – *Going back hundreds of years.*

Whether you're a law student, a legal professional, or just someone who enjoys a good "you won't believe this" kind of story, you're in for a treat. Some of these lawsuits will make you laugh, some will leave you speechless, and some might even make you rethink everything you thought you knew about the legal system.

So buckle up, grab a coffee (or something stronger), and get ready to dive into 100 of the craziest, most ridiculous lawsuits ever filed.

Let's begin.

The Clashes of Corporate Giants

Company vs. Company

Fruits, words, shoe soles, swiping features, and even Klingon—corporate lawsuits are anything but dull. Big brands will fight over the quirkiest things to keep their legal teams busy (and their fees justified). These clashes will make you laugh, but they also spark serious debates. Can you really own a color? Is a measurement trademarkable? Should a fictional language belong to a corporation?

Here are some of the most intriguing company-vs.-company lawsuits in legal history:

1. Apple vs. Prepear: A Juicy Trademark Tale

Potato, potahto. Apple, pear. Who knew a humble fruit could cause such drama? When Natalie Monson, the owner of Prepear—a recipe and meal-planning app—filed for a trademark, she probably didn't expect to go toe-to-toe with the tech giant Apple. However, as soon as her pear-shaped logo hit the trademark office, Apple jumped to claim the design was too close to their iconic bitten apple.

Apple's issue? The pear logo's leaf had a suspiciously similar right angle. Apple argued it could confuse consumers, though Prepear was, ironically, nowhere near competing in the tech giant's orbit. Monson launched a petition to rally support against the legal Goliath, and over 250,000 people joined the cause.

Fast forward to 2021, and the case wrapped up with Prepear tweaking its logo—angling the leaf just enough to make Apple happy. The app icon got a mini makeover, and Prepear's CEO called the matter "amicably resolved." While Prepear was satisfied with the outcome, the case left a sour taste that sparked debates about trademark bullying.

2. Apple Corps vs. Apple Computer: A Tale of Two Apples

Before there was Apple Computer, there was Apple Corps—the Beatles' own company. Founded to shelter millions from taxes, it took its name from a clever pun on "core." The idea came from a René Magritte painting of an apple that Paul McCartney adored. But what began as a lighthearted nod to fruit turned into a decades-long legal drama.

In 1978, Apple Corps sued Apple Computer, accusing the tech upstart of infringing on their trademark. The case ended with a 1981 settlement: Apple Computer agreed to pay $80,000 and promised to stay out of the music business. It seemed simple enough, but cracks appeared quickly. By the late '80s, Apple's computers were being used for music, which reignited the feud.

In 1991, Apple Corps filed another lawsuit. This time, Apple Computer paid $26.5 million to settle. Once again, the tech company agreed to steer clear of music. But history repeated itself. With the launch of iTunes in 2003, Apple Corps cried foul and filed yet another suit.

The 2006 trial ended in Apple Computer's favor. The court ruled that delivering music wasn't the same as producing it. Apple Corps paid legal fees, and Apple Computer secured the right to the name—for $26.8 million.

In 2007, Apple Computer rebranded as Apple Inc. The era of the "Big Apple" had officially begun.

3. Facebook vs. Teachbook: The Battle of the Books

Did you know that when you're a tech goliath, you might feel entitled to own words? Well, that's at least the case with Facebook, which sued Teachbook in 2010—a social network for teachers—claiming that the use of "-book" infringed on its trademark. Facebook argued that Teachbook was "riding the coattails" of its global fame and goodwill.

The dispute was more about branding than a name, though. Teachbook had marketed itself as a safer, teacher-friendly alternative to Facebook, even highlighting how some schools banned educators from using mainstream platforms like Facebook and MySpace. Facebook saw this as a direct challenge. A spokesperson declared, "They can create an online network for teachers, and we wish them well. What they can't do is trade on our name or dilute our brand."

Teachbook, perhaps realizing it couldn't outmuscle Facebook's legal team, opted for the easier route: rebranding. Rather than endure a drawn-out court battle, the platform quietly stepped away from its "-book" identity.

This lawsuit showcased Facebook's determination to protect its brand—even down to its suffix. It was a small victory for the tech giant, but for Teachbook, it was a lesson in picking battles.

4. Tinder vs. Bumble: Swipe Right for Drama

Love hurts, especially in the world of dating apps. In 2018, Tinder's parent company, Match Group, sued Bumble, accusing Bumble of copying its signature swipe-to-match functionality and other design elements.

However, this lawsuit, in part, was motivated by personal reasons. Bubble is co-founded by Whitney Wolfe, a former Tinder executive who left after filing a sexual discrimination lawsuit against Tinder. The history between the two companies was messier than a bad first date.

Match had previously tried to acquire Bumble for $450 million, but the bid fell flat. Some speculated that the *lawsuit was a strategic move to pressure Bumble to join forces. Bumble didn't flinch. Instead, it fired back with a $400 million countersuit, accusing Match of intimidation and fraud.*

The legal battle dragged on for two years. In June 2020, the apps finally swiped left on litigation. The settlement terms were kept under wraps, but the agreement allowed both companies to move forward independently.

In the end, the case highlighted that in the tech world, breakups can be just as messy as business deals.

5. Subway vs. Casey's General Stores: The Footlong Feud

Think Facebook trying to own "book" was a stretch? In 2010, Subway tried to trademark the measurement "footlong." The company went after Casey's General Stores, claiming the term "footlong" was theirs to own. Casey's wasn't having it.

Casey's, a Midwest-based chain, filed a lawsuit in federal court, asking for clarity: could Subway really claim exclusive rights to a word that simply describes a 12-inch sandwich? Casey's argued that "footlong" was as generic as calling a drink "thirst-quenching." In their view, Subway's claims were ridiculous.

Casey's wanted the court to declare "footlong" a generic term, free for anyone slinging subs to use. They also labeled Subway's trademark effort as "frivolous litigation."

The battle brought a touch of humor to the courtroom. After all, can you really own a measurement? The case highlighted the tension between protecting trademarks and letting everyday terms stay, well, every day.

The Trademark Trial and Appeal Board of the U.S. Patent and Trademark Office ultimately rejected Subway's application to trademark "footlong." The board ruled that the term was generic and, therefore, not eligible for trademark protection.

Casey's deserves credit for protecting sandwich menus from corporate interference.

6. Qualitex vs. Jacobson Products: The Feud Over Green-Gold

A company can't own a measurement. How about a color? This quirky legal saga began with a shade of green-gold, a color Qualitex had been using for years on its dry-cleaning press pads. These pads were recognizable, thanks to their unique hue. But in 1989, rival Jacobson Products started selling similar pads in the same green-gold color.

Qualitex wasn't impressed. They argued that the color was part of their brand identity. So, they sued Jacobson for unfair competition in federal court. To strengthen their case, Qualitex registered the color with the U.S.

Patent and Trademark Office in 1991 and tacked on a trademark infringement claim.

The District Court sided with Qualitex, agreeing that their signature shade deserved protection. But the Ninth Circuit Court of Appeals threw a wrench in the case. Their verdict? Color alone couldn't be trademarked.

This wasn't the end. The case eventually reached the U.S. Supreme Court, which ruled that color could indeed function as a trademark if it identified a product's source.

So, Qualitex won their green-gold rights and proved that in the world of trademarks, a color can carry some serious legal weight.

7. Star Trek vs. the Klingon Language: A Galactic Legal Clash

To boldly sue where no one has sued before. In 2015, Paramount Pictures and CBS found themselves in a legal battle over the Klingon language. It all started when Axanar Productions, a fan group, created a Star Trek-inspired film called Prelude to Axanar. The project included Klingon dialogue, and that's where things got tricky.

Paramount and CBS, the studios behind Star Trek, argued that Klingon was their intellectual property. They claimed the language, created for the franchise, couldn't be used without permission. Axanar

Productions fought back with a surprising defense: can a language really be owned? After all, Klingon had grown beyond its Star Trek roots, with enthusiasts learning it, translating works like Shakespeare, and even hosting Klingon-speaking conventions.

While the courts didn't directly rule on the ownership of Klingon, the case ultimately settled, with Axanar agreeing to limitations on its project.

In the end, the lawsuit left fans wondering: does the spirit of Star Trek, a universe built on exploration and creativity, align with corporate control? Qapla' (good luck) to whoever dares to answer.

8. Jack Daniel's vs. VIP Products: Whisky Meets Woof

What happens when a dog toy company takes a playful jab at a whiskey brand? You get a legal showdown mixing parody with trademark law. Jack Daniel's sued VIP Products over their "Bad Spaniels Silly Squeaker" toy, a parody of their iconic whiskey bottle. The toy mimicked the black label and fonts, with humorous text about "43% poo by volume." Unsurprisingly, Jack Daniel's wasn't laughing.

VIP Products argued it was all in good fun. They even added a tag to the toy, clarifying it wasn't affiliated with Jack Daniel's. But the whiskey giant didn't buy it. They claimed the toy diluted their brand and could mislead consumers.

The lawsuit went all the way to the U.S. Supreme Court. In 2023, the court sided with Jack Daniel's, ruling that parody doesn't give free rein to mimic trademarks when it risks damaging the brand's reputation.

This case set a precedent for how far parody can go before stepping on trademark rights. Lesson learned: not all jokes land well in court.

9. Caterpillar vs. Cat & Cloud Coffee: A Purrplexing Trademark Disagreement

What could bulldozers and coffee possibly have in common? Just one word: "cat." That was enough for construction giant Caterpillar Inc. to sue Cat & Cloud, a Santa Cruz coffee shop, for using "cat" on their clothing line.

Caterpillar argued that Cat & Cloud's apparel infringed on their trademark, which features "CAT" with a yellow triangle beneath the "A." Cat & Cloud, whose name references an actual feline (not construction equipment), called the move heavy-handed. Their logo, after all, is as different from Caterpillar's branding as an espresso machine is from an excavator.

The coffee shop, which trademarked its name in 2015, accused Caterpillar of "trademark bullying." It claimed the construction company regularly targets small businesses that lack the resources for lengthy legal fights. Despite the David vs. Goliath vibe, Cat &

Cloud stood its ground. In 2020, Caterpillar eventually withdrew its opposition and allowed the coffee shop to continue its operations—and its merch—without further interference.

The case left a bitter taste, but Cat & Cloud brewed up a win for small businesses everywhere. Sometimes, the little guy really can claw their way to victory.

10. McDonald's vs. Supermac's: The Combat of the Macs

Who says a small Irish takeaway can't stand up to a global burger powerhouse? In a nearly decade-long battle, Supermac's, a family-owned chain, took on McDonald's, the creator of the world-famous Big Mac, in a legal fight that shook the fast-food world.

The drama kicked off in 2015 when Supermac's applied to register its name in the EU to expand beyond Ireland. McDonald's wasn't lovin' it. The fast-food giant argued that "Supermac" was too similar to "Big Mac" and might confuse customers. Initially, McDonald's scored a win, preventing Supermac's from trademarking some of its menu items. But the Irish chain didn't back down. Instead, it struck back by filing with the EU Intellectual Property Office to challenge McDonald's exclusive rights to the "Big Mac" trademark.

Supermac's claimed McDonald's wasn't actively using the trademark as required by EU law and accused the American company of trademark bullying.

In 2023, the European Court of Justice agreed. The court revoked McDonald's exclusive claim to "Big Mac" in the EU and even ruled it couldn't use the name on chicken burgers.

Take that McDefeated!

11. Sambucks vs. Starbucks: The Brew-Haha Over a Name

Sambucks? Starbucks? Do the names sound alike? That's what Starbucks thought.

When Oregon coffee shop owner Sam Buck opened her café, she named it Sambuck's—a clever nod to her own name. Charming? Not to Starbucks! They claimed the name, written as one word, sounded too similar to their own.

At first, Starbucks kept it civil. They offered Sam $500 to rebrand her shop and avoid any confusion. But Sam wasn't interested. She argued that her name was her identity and that her shop wasn't trying to imitate anyone. Starbucks disagreed and decided to take the matter to court.

The coffee giant claimed that not only was the name too close for comfort, but Sambuck's logo also resembled Starbucks' iconic green branding. A coincidence? The court didn't think so. The judge ruled against Sam and ordered her to remove "Buck" from her business name, along with any branded items like coffee cups and signage.

Sam's legal fight came with a steep price tag and left her with hefty legal fees and no choice but to rebrand. Even if your intentions are innocent, going toe-to-toe with a corporate giant can be a costly brew.

12. McDonald's vs. Hungry Jack's: The Big Battle

A sesame seed bun, two beef patties, lettuce, pickles, cheese, and a middle slice of bread. Is it McDonald's or Hungry Jack's? Turns out, it's both—sort of.

When Hungry Jack's launched its "Big Jack" burger in Australia, McDonald's slapped Hungry Jack's with a trademark infringement lawsuit.

McDonald's argued that "Big Jack" could confuse customers and infringe on their trademarks for both the Big Mac and Mega Mac. Hungry Jack's didn't back down. Instead, they fired up an ad campaign claiming the Big Jack was superior. The claim became part of the courtroom drama when the meat was found not to be 25% bigger than its rival's as promoted.

For over three years, the battle of the burgers sizzled in court. McDonald's sought damages, an order to destroy all Big Jack branding, and a declaration that Hungry Jack's had crossed the line. But in the end, the judge sided with Hungry Jack's, ruling the Big Jack name did not violate McDonald's trademarks.

A whopper of a win for Hungry Jack's!

13. DeLorean vs. NBCUniversal: A Time-Traveling Trademark Tussle

The DeLorean, the time machine that made Back to the Future iconic, found itself in the middle of a legal drama that rivaled its on-screen adventures.

In December 2022, the DeLorean Motor Company (DMC) filed a lawsuit against NBCUniversal, claiming the studio owed royalties for decades of merchandise featuring the famous car. According to DMC, an agreement from 1989 required NBCUniversal to pay 5% of merchandise sales involving the DeLorean—but those payments had seemingly disappeared into the past.

NBCUniversal argued that the car's fame was tied to the movie, not the manufacturer. DMC, however, insisted the car was a star in its own right, cruising through generations of merchandise, from toys to video games. With both sides refusing to yield, the battle for royalties became heated.

In March 2024, the lawsuit ended with a confidential settlement. While the details remain under wraps, both sides agreed the DeLorean would continue to shine in Back to the Future merchandise.

This case was a reminder that intellectual property disputes can be as complicated as time travel.

14. Dyson vs. Samsung: A High-Suction Showdown

When it comes to vacuums, Dyson doesn't mess around.

In 2013, the British company took aim at Samsung. It claimed its "Motion Sync" vacuum cleaner had a steering mechanism suspiciously similar to Dyson's patented design. The tech in question was a sleek system that allowed better maneuverability, letting vacuums glide around corners like Formula 1 racers on a track.

Dyson filed a lawsuit that accused Samsung of swiping their innovation. Samsung, however, fired back by labeling Dyson a "patent troll." The term stung, especially since Dyson prides itself on being an inventor-driven company. Samsung came prepared with evidence of "prior art," arguing that similar designs existed before Dyson's patent.

The legal dust storm didn't last long. Faced with Samsung's defense, Dyson dropped the case. While the British vacuum maker didn't secure a win, they made a clear statement about how seriously they protect their tech.

This battle of the brands showcased the high stakes of innovation in home appliances. In the end, it was less about dirt and more about ideas.

15. Barbie vs. Bratz: The Ultimate Dollhouse Throwdown

Barbie may be the queen of the doll world, but even royalty faces challenges. In the early 2000s, Mattel took MGA Entertainment to court, claiming Bratz, the trendsetting newcomers, were actually the brainchild of designer Carter Bryant during his time at Mattel.

The legal war was messy. In 2008, Mattel scored a massive $100 million win and even got a court order to stop Bratz production. But MGA wasn't backing down. They appealed, and in 2011, the Ninth Circuit flipped the script. The court ruled that MGA could keep the Bratz line alive, stating that ideas—like sassy dolls with oversized heads—weren't automatically owned by Mattel.

The case spanned years, cost millions, and became a masterclass in the complexities of intellectual property law. The takeaway? Even in the world of dolls, creativity and legal battles aren't child's play.

16. Nike vs. MSCHF: The "Satan Shoes" Showdown

In March 2021, Brooklyn-based art collective MSCHF collaborated with rapper Lil Nas X to release "Satan Shoes," a series of 666 modified Nike Air Max 97 sneakers. These black and red shoes featured a pentagram charm, the inscription "LUKE 10:18," and a drop of human blood in the sole. Priced at $1,018, they sold out in under a minute.

Nike, however, concerned about brand confusion and unauthorized use of its trademark, filed a lawsuit against MSCHF. The court granted Nike a temporary restraining order, which halted further sales.

In April 2021, both parties reached a settlement. MSCHF agreed to a voluntary recall and offered refunds to purchasers to remove the shoes from circulation. This case underscores the complexities of trademark law and the tensions between artistic expression and brand protection.

17. Anheuser-Busch vs. Budweiser Budvar: The Clash of the Buds

Two breweries. One name. A century-long clash over who gets to rule the beer kingdom.

For more than 100 years, Anheuser-Busch InBev (AB InBev) from the U.S. and Czech-based Budějovický Budvar have battled over the rights to the "Budweiser" name. Both claim historical ties. Budvar comes from České Budějovice (Budweis), a town famous for its brewing heritage. AB InBev, on the other hand, built a global empire on its Budweiser brand.

This is no small fight. It's a global legal war with over 100 disputes around the world. In Europe, Budvar usually wins, keeping the name "Budweiser." Meanwhile, AB InBev sells its beer there as "Bud." But in North America, AB InBev holds the upper hand.

One of the most notable battles happened in Italy. In 2013, after years of legal back-and-forth, the Italian

Supreme Court ruled that AB InBev's use of "Budweiser" was misleading. The court removed AB InBev's trademark, giving Budvar the right to use the name in Italy.

The takeaway? In beer wars, tradition and branding can be as powerful as the brew itself.

18. Christian Louboutin vs. Yves Saint Laurent: Red Sole Showdown

It was a clash of the soles.

In 2011, Christian Louboutin, the king of the red-bottomed stiletto, took Yves Saint Laurent (YSL) to court. The drama began when YSL released an all-red shoe, complete with crimson soles. For Louboutin, whose red sole had been trademarked since 2008, this was a step too far. He argued that the red sole was his signature, a design so iconic it practically screamed "Louboutin."

YSL, however, claimed red soles were nothing new and had been used in fashion long before Louboutin made them famous. The real question became: Can a color be owned? The legal battle strutted into the courtroom, with Louboutin demanding damages and an injunction to stop YSL from using red soles altogether.

In 2012, the U.S. Court of Appeals delivered its verdict. Louboutin's red sole trademark was valid—but only when paired with a contrasting upper color. YSL's monochromatic red shoes didn't infringe, meaning they were free to walk the runway. Both brands claimed victory, but the ruling proved that in fashion, even the soles can spark a high-stakes debate.

19. Wham-O vs. Manley Toys: A Splash of Yellow Justice

Another courtroom drama over a color—this time, sunshine yellow.

In 2007, Wham-O, the maker of the beloved Slip 'N Slide, found itself sliding into a legal battle with ToyQuest (SLB Toys USA). ToyQuest's water slides were sporting Wham-O's signature yellow.

Wham-O claimed ToyQuest's use of yellow was a deliberate attempt to ride on their brand's decades-long success. For Wham-O, yellow was a symbol of fun, nostalgia, and childhood summers.

A San Francisco jury agreed. They ruled that ToyQuest had willfully infringed on Wham-O's trademark, engaged in false advertising, and diluted the value of its iconic branding. ToyQuest was ordered to pay Wham-O $6 million in damages.

Mojde Esfandiari, Wham-O's CEO, called the decision a win for both the company and its loyal customers. She vowed to protect Wham-O's iconic yellow slide from any imitators.

Wham-O showed that when it comes to trademarks, they won't just let things slide.

20. Lego vs. Guangdong Loongon: The Fight of the Bricks

LEGO is the undisputed king of building blocks. However, in the mid-2010s, a challenger appeared—Lepin, a Chinese company that copied LEGO's designs almost exactly. In 2016, LEGO fought back, suing Lepin's parent company, Shantou Meizhi Model Co., for copyright infringement and unfair competition.

In 2018, the Guangzhou Intellectual Property Court ruled in LEGO's favor. Lepin was ordered to stop production and pay damages.

The battle didn't stop there. In April 2019, Shanghai police raided Lepin's factories, seizing assets and arresting key executives. This was a major blow to Lepin's operations. By January 2020, LEGO had fully won the fight. The court reaffirmed its earlier decision, awarding LEGO around RMB 4.7 million in damages and requiring Lepin to issue public apologies.

21. McDonald's vs. Quality Inns International: The Fight Over "McSleep"

Let's say you're booking a hotel while traveling across the country. A name pops up: McSleep Inn. Would you assume it's connected to McDonald's? If your answer is yes, then McDonald's might have been right to complain.

In the late 1980s, Quality Inns International had a dream—a new budget hotel chain called "McSleep

Inn." But before they could fluff the pillows, McDonald's woke them up with a lawsuit. The fast-food giant argued that the "Mc" in "McSleep Inn" was too close to their trademarked family of "Mc" products, like McNuggets and McMuffins.

Quality Inns fought back, asking the court for a ruling that "McSleep Inn" didn't infringe on McDonald's trademarks. McDonald's countered with claims of trademark infringement and unfair competition. The court sided with the burger giant, stating that the "Mc" prefix had become synonymous with McDonald's in the public's mind. Using "McSleep Inn," the court ruled, could confuse customers into thinking they were booking a room in the house of Ronald McDonald.

In the end, Quality Inns ditched the name and went back to the drawing board, eventually coming up with Sleep Inn.

22. Sid & Marty Krofft Television Productions Inc. vs. McDonald's Corp.: The Battle of the Puppets

It's always funny to watch corporations sue over a name, only to turn around and swipe creative ideas for themselves.

In the 1970s, Sid and Marty Krofft, creators of the fantastical children's show H.R. Pufnstuf, saw something suspicious. McDonald's had rolled out a series of "McDonaldland" commercials featuring quirky characters and enchanted settings. Those characters and settings looked an awful lot like the ones from H.R. Pufnstuf. From talking trees to colorful puppets, the resemblance was downright blatant.

The Kroffts didn't take it lying down. In 1971, they filed a lawsuit against McDonald's, claiming the fast-food giant had ripped off their work. The case went to trial, and in 1977, the court sided with the Kroffts.

The court awarded the Kroffts $50,000 in damages—not exactly a supersized payout, but a moral victory nonetheless. More importantly, the case set a legal precedent. It showed that creative work, no matter how whimsical, deserved serious protection.

23. National Biscuit Company vs. Kellogg Company: The Breakfast Conflict

If you think the cereal aisle is all sweetness, think again—it's had its share of salty moments.

In the 1930s, the National Biscuit Company (NBC), known today as Nabisco, had been producing shredded wheat since the early 1900s. They owned the patents for both the iconic pillow-shaped cereal and the machinery that made it. But when those patents expired, Kellogg jumped into the bowl.

Kellogg began making its own shredded wheat, using the same name and familiar shape. NBC claimed that "shredded wheat" was their brand. Kellogg, they argued, was confusing customers and nibbling away at their market share. The case went all the way to the U.S. Supreme Court in 1938.

The court had a lot to chew on. Was "shredded wheat" a trademark or a generic term? Was the pillow shape functional or brand-defining? Ultimately, the court ruled for Kellogg. The term "shredded wheat" was generic, the shape was purely functional, and Kellogg's packaging was different enough to avoid confusion.

This landmark ruling declared that once a patent expires, the innovation belongs to everyone.

24. Getty Images vs. Stability AI: A Picture-Perfect Legal Battle

In early 2023, a copyright showdown broke out between Getty Images, the stock photo giant, and Stability AI, the brains behind the popular AI image generator, Stable Diffusion.

Getty claimed Stability AI had lifted millions of its copyrighted photos without permission to train their AI model. Adding insult to injury, some of the generated images even included traces of Getty's watermark.

Getty argued that Stability AI had violated intellectual property laws and skipped paying for a proper license. Stability AI fired back, claiming fair use and insisting that training their model on existing images was just part of the AI innovation game.

The case is currently in the hands of the High Court in London and has the tech and creative worlds on edge. The outcome could shape the future of AI training and copyright law. If Getty wins, AI developers might have to secure pricey licenses for datasets, potentially slowing innovation. If Stability AI wins, it could open the door for broader data use in AI.

Stay tuned as the legal brushstrokes complete this high-stakes picture.

25. Puma vs. Adidas: A Sibling Rivalry

Once upon a time in Herzogenaurach, Germany, two brothers, Adolf (Adi) and Rudolf (Rudi) Dassler, teamed up to create athletic shoes. Their company, Dassler Brothers Shoe Company, even outfitted athletes in the 1936 Olympics. But this tale of teamwork didn't last. By the end of World War II, their partnership fell apart over personal and professional tensions. And so began one of the fiercest rivalries in sportswear history.

In 1948, Rudi stormed off to start Puma, and Adi countered by founding Adidas a year later. The brothers didn't just split the family—they split the entire town. Herzogenaurach became a battleground, with locals choosing sides. Even local sports teams and shops aligned with one brother or the other.

Adidas gained global fame in 1954 when the West German football team won the World Cup wearing its boots. Not to be outdone, Puma scored big with star endorsements, including football legend Pelé during the 1970 World Cup. The competition between the two brands revolutionized sports marketing, athlete sponsorships, and footwear design.

Though the brothers have long passed, their rivalry lives on. Adidas and Puma remain global giants, proving that even a bitter feud can leave a legacy.

Taking on the Corporate World

Wrong weather forecasts, over-the-top haunted house scares, and $54 million pants—these lawsuits prove there's no limit to what people will sue companies over. They also teach us some quirky lessons like: always carry an umbrella, check your food labels twice, and never underestimate a customer's love for their trousers. Dive into these tales of courtroom drama, where absurdity and legal battles collide.

1. Caught in the Rain

The English got it right: carry an umbrella, and it won't rain. A woman in Haifa skipped hers after hearing weather forecaster Danny Rup promise a sunny, clear day. But nature had other plans. Rain poured, storms rolled in, and the woman found herself dressed for summer in the middle of a downpour.

She blamed Rup's sunny forecast for her misfortune. Without proper clothing or shelter, she claims she caught the flu, missed four days of work, and had to spend $38 on medication. On top of that, she endured stress from the entire ordeal. Frustrated, she decided to take action. Her demands were simple: financial compensation for her troubles and an apology from Rup.

She got both. The TV station settled the case out of court, paying her $1,000 and issuing a formal apology. We have all something to learn from this lawsuit: don't rely entirely on the weatherman, and always have an umbrella handy.

2. Halloween Horror at Universal Studios

Life is full of expectations. See dark clouds? Expect rain. Spot a hole in an apple? Don't be surprised to find a worm. Step into a haunted house? You're signing up to be scared. But for one woman in Orlando, the scares at Universal Studios went too far.

Peters attended Universal Studios' Halloween Horror Nights with her 10-year-old granddaughter. She expected thrills and maybe a few laughs. Instead, she claims the experience left her emotionally distressed. The trouble began as they exited one of the haunted house attractions. An actor dressed as Leatherface from The Texas Chainsaw Massacre chased them with a roaring chainsaw.

Things took a turn when Peters and her granddaughter slipped on a wet floor and fell. But instead of offering help, the Leatherface actor reportedly stood over them, continuing the act.

Feeling traumatized, Peters decided to sue Universal Studios. She sought $15,000 for emotional distress and negligence. After multiple trials, the court ruled in her favor. She received compensation, but the actor faced no consequences for his role.

In the end, Universal learned that scares might come at a price.

3. Pepsi and the Harrier Jet Courtroom Drama

Be careful of what you promise, even as a joke. Pepsi learned this the hard way in 1996. In a playful commercial for its Pepsi Points loyalty program, the brand featured a Harrier jet as a prize for collecting 7 million points. Most people got the joke. But John Leonard, a 21-year-old business student, didn't laugh—he took it seriously.

The ad showed a jet swooping into a schoolyard, and Leonard did the math. He discovered Pepsi allowed points to be purchased for 10¢ each. With this loophole, he raised $700,008.50 and mailed the check to Pepsi, demanding his jet, worth $37.4 million. Pepsi declined, saying the offer was meant as a joke. Leonard sued, claiming the ad constituted a binding contract.

In response, Pepsi adjusted the ad and raised the jet's cost to 700 million points. Meanwhile, the court wasn't impressed with Leonard's argument. It ruled in Pepsi's favor, stating no reasonable person would believe the ad seriously offered a fighter jet.

Leonard didn't win, but his case became a legendary example of taking marketing a little too literally.

4. The Footlong Fiasco

Know your audience before you advertise. It's the golden rule of marketing. Subway seemed to miss that memo when it promoted its "footlong" sandwich. They didn't expect someone like Matt Corby, an Australian teenager, to pull out a ruler and measure the sandwich. But he did. His discovery? The footlong was only 11 inches, not 12.

Maybe Matt wasn't familiar with the quirks of bread-baking. Bread, like the weather, doesn't always behave predictably. Natural variations can impact its size. But that didn't matter. When Matt posted his findings on social media, the internet went wild. A group of consumers then launched a class action lawsuit against Subway, claiming false advertising.

Subway eventually agreed to settle. The terms were that they would inspect and measure their bread to ensure all sandwiches met the 12-inch promise, and they would pay over half a million dollars in attorney fees. However, in a twist, the U.S. Court of Appeals for the Seventh Circuit rejected the settlement. The court ruled it wasn't fair or beneficial to Subway customers. Instead, the deal seemed to only reward the lawyers involved.

5. The Case of the $54 Million Pants

Did you know that a lost pair of pants could equal $54 million in emotional distress? Roy Pearson must have really loved those trousers because when his dry cleaner lost them, he took them to court. On the *witness stand, Pearson broke down in tears and had to pause his testimony when things got too emotional—while questioning himself, no less. Referring to himself as "we," Pearson claimed to be leading a class of thousands, possibly hundreds of thousands, who he said were at risk of being duped by the store's "Satisfaction Guaranteed" and "Same-Day Service" signs.*

A quick recap: On May 3, 2005, Pearson dropped off a pair of gray pants at Custom Cleaners, a dry cleaning shop in DC run by Jin, Soo, and Ki Chung. When the pants came back, Pearson claimed they weren't his. He demanded $1,000 as compensation, which the Chungs refused. Pearson responded by suing them for $67 million, later "slashing" his demand to $54 million.

The court wasn't convinced. Pearson lost the lawsuit and his subsequent appeal. The Chungs, initially seeking to recover legal fees, dropped their request after raising funds through a community campaign. The case became a symbol of excessive litigation and remains one of the most infamous examples of taking grievances a step too far.

6. The Nugget That Cost $800,000

McDonald's could fill a whole library with the lawsuits filed against it. Over the years, the fast-food giant has faced its fair share of legal troubles. In 2019, one such case centered around a dangerously hot chicken nugget.

Philana Holmes visited a McDonald's in Tamarac, Florida, with her 4-year-old daughter Olivia. During the meal, a chicken nugget fell onto Olivia's thighs, causing second-degree burns. Attorneys for Holmes claimed the nuggets were served at over 200 degrees Fahrenheit, while McDonald's argued the high temperature was necessary to prevent salmonella.

A South Florida jury ruled McDonald's and the franchise owner, Upchurch Foods, were liable for failing to warn customers about potential harm from the hot nuggets. However, only Upchurch was found negligent for the burns. The jury awarded Olivia $800,000 in damages for the injuries she suffered.

This case reminded everyone that sometimes, fast food can be a little too hot to handle.

7. When a CAT Scan Crossed the Psychic Line

For all you psychics out there, avoid CAT scans. According to Judith Richardson Haimes, they'll strip away your powers—or at least that's what she claimed in court. Haimes argued that a CAT scan caused her to suffer debilitating headaches whenever she tried to focus on using her psychic abilities.

Before the scan, Haimes said she made a living as a psychic. She claimed to read people's auras and even assist police with solving crimes. However, after undergoing a procedure at Temple University Hospital, she alleged an allergic reaction to the iodine tracer used for the scan. This, she said, robbed her of her psychic gifts and her ability to earn a living.

Her attorney argued the case, and a jury awarded Haimes over $600,000 for pain, suffering, and lost income. However, the victory didn't last. On appeal, the award was overturned, leaving Haimes without the compensation she sought.

8. The $340 Million Powerball Error

The odds of hitting the Powerball jackpot are slim—one in 292.2 million. For comparison, you're far more likely to be struck by lightning (1 in 1.22 million). In January 2023, John Cheeks thought he had defied those odds. For a brief moment, he believed he was a $340 million winner. But his celebration didn't last long.

Cheeks bought his ticket on January 6 and later saw his numbers posted as the winning combination on the DC Lottery website. Overjoyed, he headed to the Office of Lottery and Gaming (OLG) to claim his prize. That's where the dream ended. OLG administrators denied his claim, explaining the posted numbers were a mistake caused by a technical glitch.

According to court documents, a quality assurance team working for the contractor Taoti Enterprises accidentally uploaded test numbers to the live website instead of a private development site. These incorrect numbers went live on January 6, a day before the actual drawing, and remained visible until January 9.

Cheeks refused to accept the error and is now suing for $340 million, including daily interest.

The lawsuit is still ongoing, but for now, Cheeks remains a potential millionaire waiting for justice.

9. Sugar or Cane Juice?

Does "evaporated cane juice" sound like something healthy? Jessica Gomez thought so. In 2017, she filed a class-action lawsuit against Jelly Belly Candy Company, accusing them of misleading consumers with their labeling of "Sport Beans." Instead of calling it what it was—sugar—the company used the term "evaporated cane juice," which Gomez claimed duped health-conscious buyers into believing the product was sugar-free.

The product in question, Sport Beans, is marketed to athletes as a source of carbohydrates, electrolytes, and vitamins. Gomez alleged that avoiding the word "sugar" was no accident. She argued it was a deliberate move to appeal to health-conscious consumers while disguising the true nature of the product.

In May 2016, the FDA updated its guidelines, stating that "evaporated cane juice" is misleading and that "juice" should only describe fruits or vegetables. While the FDA's guidance isn't legally binding, it sparked a wave of lawsuits against brands using the term.

The outcome of Gomez's case remains unclear. However, her lawsuit shines a spotlight on the tricky world of food labeling and the fine line between clever marketing and consumer deception.

10. The Case of the Missing Mints

Who hasn't felt a little cheated opening a candy box with more air than candy? For Biola Daniel of New York City, the disappointment was serious enough to file a lawsuit against Tootsie Roll Industries. She claimed a box of Junior Mints purchased at a Duane Reade store contained about 40% air.

She wasn't alone. Two other plaintiffs, Abel Duran and Trekeela Perkins, joined the case. They argued the candy maker was misleading customers into thinking the boxes contained more candy than they actually did. The amended class-action lawsuit accused Junior Mints of inflating the product's value by leaving excessive empty space, or "slack-fill," in their packaging.

While some slack-fill is functional—used to protect products, allow for settling during shipping, or assist in manufacturing—the plaintiffs claimed Junior Mints had more air than other candies of similar size and shape.

In the end, U.S. District Judge Naomi Reice Buchwald dismissed the case. She ruled that "reasonable" consumers could easily determine the weight and candy count from the box labeling and would naturally expect some empty space.

11. When All-Weather Shoes Can't Handle the Weather

When your all-weather, waterproof shoes don't live up to the hype, what's the next step? For some frustrated customers, it's taking legal action.

In November 2022, Crocs found itself at the center of a class-action lawsuit filed in the U.S. District Court for the Northern District of California. Plaintiffs claim that the company's footwear, made from its proprietary Croslite material, shrinks when exposed to heat, sunlight, or water. According to the lawsuit, this shrinkage leaves the shoes unusable, directly contradicting Crocs' marketing as durable, water-friendly footwear.

By June 2023, Crocs filed motions to dismiss the amended complaint, which accused them of fraudulent concealment, misrepresentation, and false advertising. They also sought to strike the class allegations. But in April 2024, a federal judge denied these motions, allowing the case to move forward.

The plaintiffs' attorneys argue that Crocs failed to disclose critical information about the shoes' potential to shrink under normal conditions. They believe this omission misled consumers who trusted the product's durability and suitability for outdoor and water activities.

As this lawsuit unfolds, it highlights the importance of honesty in product advertising. Buyers expect durability and transparency, especially for items marketed as tough and weather-resistant. For now, the case stands as a lesson in the value of truth in marketing.

12. The Spicy Case of Texas Pete

Can hot sauce be falsely advertised? According to Phillip White of California, the answer was yes. In September 2022, White filed a lawsuit against TW Garner Food Company, claiming their Texas Pete hot sauce was misleadingly marketed as being from Texas. The product, he argued, wasn't connected to the Lone Star State at all. Instead, it's made in North Carolina, where the company is headquartered.

White alleged that the name and branding, complete with a cowboy and lone star, tricked consumers into believing it was a Texas-made product. He claimed he would've paid less for the sauce had he known its true origins. White even asked the court to force Texas Pete to change its name.

At first, a judge appeared to side with White, noting that consumers could reasonably assume the product was made in Texas. But the company stood firm. They pointed out that the label clearly identified its North Carolina origins and emphasized the historical story behind the name.

In September 2023, White abruptly dropped the lawsuit, and the case was dismissed.

13. The Lemon Lawsuit That Turned Sour

What do you expect when you see lemons on a drink label? Jeanne Matthews and Timothy Alexander assumed they were buying water flavored with real lemons. Instead, they found out that the lemon flavor in Poland Spring sparkling water and Polar lemon seltzer came from artificial flavoring, not the fruit itself. Disappointed and feeling misled, they filed a lawsuit against Poland Spring.

The plaintiffs argued that the packaging was designed to appeal to health-conscious consumers trying to avoid sugary drinks. Labels on both products prominently featured lemon slices and phrases like "Refreshingly Natural" and "With a Twist of Lemon." Matthews and Alexander claimed these design choices led consumers to believe the drinks contained real lemon ingredients, which provide actual nutritional value.

Instead, the lemon taste reportedly came from lab-created formulas made with fruit and vegetable essences. The plaintiffs said they wouldn't have bought the products—or at least wouldn't have paid as much—if they'd known the truth.

In the end, the case was dismissed. The judge called the dispute "a big fuss about a little lemon," leaving the plaintiffs empty-handed and perhaps a bit bitter.

14. Eye Drops or Cash Drops?

Imagine buying a bottle of eye drops advertised to last 30 days, only to find it empty by day 20. Annoying, right? But would it bother you enough to sue? In October 2022, Clark Alexandre decided it did. He filed a class-action lawsuit against Alcon Laboratories, claiming their Pataday-brand eye drops fell short of the promised duration, even when used as directed—one drop per eye daily.

According to Alexandre, this wasn't an isolated issue. A 2017 ProPublica investigation revealed that drug companies often produce eye drops larger than what a human eye can absorb. Consumers end up buying more bottles, padding the profits of drug companies. The report also highlighted that Alcon once developed a "microdrop" technology in the 1990s to minimize waste. Yet they never implemented it, allegedly because it was less profitable than selling oversized drops.

The court, however, wasn't convinced. The lawsuit was dismissed, with the judge ruling that the plaintiffs' claims—that they'd have paid less for smaller, more efficient bottles—were too speculative to meet legal standing.

This case left consumers wondering: when it comes to eye drops, are we paying for product or waste?

15. Dreaming of Spain but Landing in the Caribbean

Dr. Edward Gamson and his partner planned a luxurious getaway to Granada, Spain, in 2014, booking first-class tickets through British Airways. But a ticketing blunder turned their dream trip into a nightmare. Instead of the historic Spanish city, they were flown to Grenada, a small island in the Caribbean. The destination was correctly spelled on their tickets, but the couple didn't realize the error until 20 minutes after their flight to St. Lucia, a Caribbean layover, had taken off from London.

What followed was a chaotic three-day ordeal involving seven flights. Ultimately, they abandoned the Granada excursion and rerouted to Lisbon, Portugal, where Dr. Gamson had a conference. The mishap cost them $2,776, and Gamson decided to sue British Airways for $34,000, citing the cost of the tickets and lost wages. However, the court dismissed the case.

In hindsight, perhaps the Caribbean detour wasn't all bad—Grenada is home to some of the world's most stunning beaches, after all.

16. Pimp's $100 Million Claim Against Nike

In 2014, imprisoned pimp Sirgiorgio Sanford Clardy made headlines when he filed a $100 million lawsuit against Nike. His claim? His Air Jordan sneakers should have come with a warning label, cautioning users that they could be used as a dangerous weapon. Clardy, who was serving a 100-year prison sentence, *had brutally stomped on the face of a man who tried to leave a motel without paying for services.*

Representing himself in court, Clardy appeared via video feed from prison. While Nike's legal team used just 90 seconds to argue their case, Clardy spent most of the hearing rambling, often veering off-topic. Unsurprisingly, the court dismissed his case after he failed to prove his claim.

Though the lawsuit didn't succeed, it highlighted just how far some individuals will go to shift blame—and left people questioning whether his Air Jordans deserved any of the spotlight.

17. Viewer Sues NBC Over Rat-Eating Stunt

In 2005, NBC's Fear Factor found itself in legal hot water after an episode featuring contestants eating rats triggered a lawsuit. Cleveland resident Austin Aitken sued the network for $2.5 million, claiming the show's graphic content caused him severe distress. The controversial episode showed participants blending rats into a smoothie and drinking it—a stunt that Aitken said was so revolting that it made him vomit, become dizzy, and even temporarily disoriented.

Aitken argued that Fear Factor had crossed the line of decency, exposing viewers to grotesque and shocking content without sufficient warning. He claimed the disturbing nature of the episode directly harmed him and demanded compensation for his suffering. While some viewers had simply turned off the TV, Aitken said the images stuck with him, affecting his peace of mind.

The lawsuit, however, was swiftly dismissed. The judge ruled that while the show's content might be offensive to some, viewers had the option to avoid it and that Aitken's case lacked legal standing. Despite its failure in court, the lawsuit became a memorable moment in the history of outrageous TV-related legal claims, sparking debate over where to draw the line between entertainment and exploitation.

18. When Following Directions Leads to a Lawsuit

In today's world, it's hard to imagine navigating without Google Maps—but one woman may have taken its directions a bit too literally. In 2011, Lauren Rosenberg filed a lawsuit against Google after following walking directions that led her to cross a busy rural highway. Instead of finding an alternative path and letting Google recalculate, Rosenberg continued across the highway, where she was struck by an oncoming car. She suffered serious injuries and sued both Google—citing negligence, failure to warn, and defective design—and the driver who hit her.

The case reached the third judicial district court in Salt Lake City, where Google requested a dismissal. The judge ruled in Google's favor, stating that the company had no legal obligation to protect users from harm and that the route suggested by Google Maps was not inherently unsafe.

The decision also highlighted that pedestrians have a duty to assess risks and act responsibly. The judge noted that Rosenberg failed to provide evidence that the suggested route was more dangerous than any other. The case became a reminder that while technology is helpful, personal judgment should always play a role.

19. Batman vs. Batman

In 2008, the mayor of Batman, a small city in southeastern Turkey, took an unexpected step into the spotlight by filing a lawsuit against Warner Bros. and The Dark Knight director Christopher Nolan. His claim? That the blockbuster films had wrongfully used the town's name, causing financial and reputational harm.

The mayor argued that Batman's name, shared with the iconic DC superhero, had been used without the town's permission. He suggested that the franchise's global popularity overshadowed the small city, leading to economic distress. The lawsuit also claimed that the town had suffered from negative publicity due to the name association, though specifics were not detailed.

Located near the Tigris River, Batman is known for its oil production and unique history. The mayor's bold legal move aimed to bring attention to the town, which he believed deserved recognition—and compensation—for sharing its name with one of pop culture's most famous vigilantes.

The case garnered international headlines and sparked debates about trademarks, geography, and pop culture. Although the lawsuit ultimately didn't go anywhere, it certainly gave the town of Batman its 15 minutes of fame, leaving fans to wonder: Did the mayor want justice or just a moment in the Bat-signal's glow?

When Companies Get Angry!

Spilled secrets, cheeky parodies, piracy, and even Barbie enchiladas—companies have sued for it all. These lawsuits are filled with twists, laughs, and lessons. Dive in to discover how stepping on a company's toes—or trademark—can spark a legal showdown, and maybe pick up a tip or two along the way!

1. Microsoft vs. MikeRoweSoft

What happens when your name inspires a clever pun? If you're Mike Rowe, you turn it into a domain name: MikeRoweSoft. Seemed harmless, right? Not to Microsoft. When the Canadian teenager launched his site to promote his web design business, Microsoft hit him with a cease-and-desist letter. They even offered $10 to cover his costs. Mike, unimpressed by the offer, countered with $10,000, which Microsoft took as an admission of cybersquatting—reserving a domain to profit off someone else's trademark.

By the end of 2003, Mike decided to take his fight public, which earned him widespread support. He collected over $6,000 in donations that allowed him to seek legal help. His site skyrocketed in popularity, racking up over 250,000 daily visitors.

Faced with mounting negative publicity, Microsoft eased its position. The dispute ended with a settlement that included an Xbox, games, Microsoft certification training, a Developer Network subscription, and an all-expenses-paid trip to the Microsoft Research Tech Fest.

What began as a domain name dispute became a lesson in how public support can level the playing field, even against tech giants.

2. The Battle of the Mice

Nothing lasts forever—not even the unlikely friendship between two famous mice.

In one corner, you had Disney, with its world-famous Mickey Mouse ears. In the other, Deadmau5 (aka Joel Zimmerman), the EDM artist known for his signature mouse head helmet. What started as a collaboration turned into a legal showdown. Disney, claiming Deadmau5's logo looked too much like Mickey's iconic silhouette, argued it could confuse fans.

Deadmau5 fired back, insisting his design was completely original and had no connection to Disney. The drama was all the more surprising because the two had worked together before. Disney had licensed one of Deadmau5's tracks for a video game and even explored other joint ventures. But somewhere along the way, the relationship soured.

The lawsuit didn't see much courtroom action. Instead, both sides chose to settle privately. The exact terms of the agreement remain a mystery, but it seems both Mickey and Deadmau5 were able to hold onto their mouse-inspired looks.

For now, the battle of the mice is over, and both icons continue to rule their respective kingdoms. Let's just hope they don't cross paths at the cheese aisle.

3. The Hack That Shook the Gaming World

There's a saying that goes: if you don't want to be hacked, build a better system. Okay, maybe that's not a real saying, but it fits this story about George Hotz, aka Geohot, a 21-year-old hacker who cracked the PlayStation 3's secure operating system. Predictably, Sony didn't take this kindly and sued him for copyright infringement and fraud. Hotz's hack opened the door for users to install unauthorized software, including homebrew games. Sony feared it could also enable piracy—a major concern for the gaming giant.

Hotz insisted his actions were driven by curiosity, not to aid pirates. Sony, however, argued that his work violated their rights and compromised the integrity of their system. The case grabbed headlines, sparking debates about the balance between user rights and corporate control.

The legal drama didn't make it to trial. Instead, Sony and Hotz settled out of court. Hotz agreed to stop tinkering with Sony products, while Sony sidestepped further public scrutiny.

The case may be closed, but the questions it raised linger. Who truly owns the technology we buy: the companies or the consumers? While Sony's victory protected its systems, it reignited conversations about control in the tech world.

4. A $2.1 Million Game Over

Create a popular game. Get upset when people want to play it without paying. And better yet, sue the person keeping those players engaged. That's exactly what Nintendo did a few years ago.

In 2021, it won a $2.1 million lawsuit against Matthew Storman, the creator of ROMUniverse. The site allowed people to download illegal copies of Nintendo games, often through paid premium accounts. Storman denied uploading the files himself.

Nintendo originally asked for $15 million in damages for copyright infringement and profiting from pirated games. While the court didn't grant the full amount, it awarded Nintendo $2.15 million. Storman tried to counter-sue, claiming Nintendo's copyright claims were false, but the court dismissed his arguments.

Storman shut down ROMUniverse in 2020, and Nintendo requested a permanent ban to stop him from running similar websites. The judge denied this, saying there wasn't enough evidence that he would repeat the violations.

This lawsuit was a clear message from Nintendo that it will fight to protect its games and stop piracy. For fans of retro games, it's a reminder that while emulating games you already own is legal, sharing pirated files online is not.

5. When Fox Took a Joke Too Seriously

Can a phrase belong to one company? Fox News thought so. In 2003, the network sued comedian and author Al Franken, along with his publisher Penguin Group, for using their slogan "Fair and Balanced" in the title of his book, Lies and the Lying Liars Who Tell Them: A Fair and Balanced Look at the Right. The lawsuit demanded a title change and sought damages, claiming Franken was using their trademark to confuse readers and sell more books.

Franken and his publisher called the lawsuit an attempt to silence free speech. A spokesperson for Dutton Books even called it "un-American." The legal drama added to Franken's ongoing feud with Fox, especially with Bill O'Reilly. At a book fair, the two clashed in a heated argument. O'Reilly called Franken "vicious" and "blinded by ideology," while Franken criticized O'Reilly for making false claims about awards his old show had won.

In the end, the judge dismissed the lawsuit, ruling in Franken's favor. The book kept its title, and the case became a battle over satire, free speech, and whether a company can truly own a phrase. It left Fox with more headlines than they might have wanted.

6. South Butt vs. North Face

When your peers annoy you with their herd mentality, all wearing the same brand, you make a parody of it. That's exactly what Jimmy Winkelmann did in 2007. Frustrated by everyone's obsession with The North Face, he created his own line called The South Butt. He went a step further and even created a cheeky tagline, "Never Stop Relaxing," poking fun at The North Face's famous slogan, "Never Stop Exploring."

The parody didn't go unnoticed. The North Face wasn't laughing and filed a lawsuit and accused Winkelmann of trademark infringement. They demanded he stop selling, promoting, and producing his products and drop his trademark application. Ironically, the lawsuit only fueled interest in The South Butt. Media coverage turned the small venture into a sensation. Within 24 hours, Winkelmann's entire inventory sold out.

The case went to Missouri's federal court in 2008 and even included Williams Pharmacy, the company handling The South Butt's manufacturing. After months of legal back-and-forth, the court ordered mediation. By April 1, 2010, both sides reached a confidential settlement.

Winkelmann's parody may have started as a joke, but it became a viral success. It proved that sometimes humor is the best business strategy.

7. Activists vs. Corporate Power

Immature people often get defensive when confronted with the truth about their actions. Apparently, the same goes for companies. McDonald's took it personally when two activists, Helen Steel and Dave Morris, distributed leaflets accusing the fast-food giant of questionable practices—like exploiting workers, harming animals, and selling unhealthy food. In 1990, McDonald's sued them for libel.

The trial turned into a marathon, dragging on for 314 days. With no money for lawyers, Steel and Morris had to defend themselves. In the end, the court ruled that McDonald's had been unfairly criticized on some points but agreed their advertising was misleading and that some complaints were justified. McDonald's got a symbolic £60,000 in damages, later cut to £40,000.

The fight didn't end there. Steel and Morris took the case to the European Court of Human Rights and argued the trial wasn't fair. In 2005, the court agreed, calling out the lack of legal aid and the trial's complexity. It was a win for free speech and led to changes in UK libel laws.

8. The Parody Website That Crossed the Line

How far would you go to troll an organization you dislike? In 1995, Michael Doughney registered the domain peta.org for a parody website called "People Eating Tasty Animals." The site included links to over 30 pages promoting leather goods and meat sales. It even featured a cheeky message at the bottom: "Feeling lost? Offended? Maybe you should leave," with a link to the official People for the Ethical Treatment of Animals (PETA) website.

When PETA caught wind of the site in 1996, they asked Doughney to hand over the domain. Doughney refused, which set the stage for a legal battle. PETA accused him of trademark infringement, dilution, unfair competition, and cybersquatting.

Doughney argued the site was just a parody, protected as free speech. However, the District Court for the Eastern District of Virginia disagreed. It ruled in PETA's favor and ordered Doughney to stop using the domain and transfer it to PETA. The case showcased the tension between legal trademark rules and daring internet humor.

9. The Sneaker Drama

It was love at first sight: a sneaker customizer bursting with creativity and a company with boundless resources. But like many promising beginnings, this story ended in conflict. Nike sued Dominic "The Shoe Surgeon" Ciambrone for $60 million, alleging he copied their designs and used their trademarks without *permission. The renowned customizer, famous for creating unique shoes inspired by Nike's styles, was accused of crossing the line. Nike claimed he sold unauthorized sneakers, taught others how to replicate Nike-like designs, and misused over 30 of their trademarks.*

Nike and Ciambrone had collaborated in the past, designing custom shoes for Nike-sponsored athletes like LeBron James. However, this lawsuit centered on more recent creations, which Nike argued confused customers and damaged their brand. The company sought to halt Ciambrone's unauthorized sales and demanded compensation for damages.

Nike has handled similar disputes in the past, such as with Bape, who agreed to redesign its sneakers. Whether this case will follow a similar path remains uncertain, but it's already stirring up major buzz in the sneaker world.

10. Oops, They Sued Her Again

You'd think brands would be flattered when a major pop star features their designs in a music video. Not Louis Vuitton! In 2007, the French luxury brand took Sony BMG and MTV Online to court over the "Do Somethin'" video, where Britney drives a pink car with the unmistakable "LV" logo plastered on the dashboard.

The lawsuit, filed in Paris, claimed the unauthorized logo appearance "damaged their image." The court *agreed because nothing screams "brand tarnish" like Britney bopping to her own song in a glittery ride. Sony BMG and MTV Online were hit with $117,000 fines each, plus undisclosed legal fees. For added drama, the video was banned in Europe.*

Years later, the music video reappeared in a sanitized, logo-free version. This time, it made sure no designer handbags were harmed. Lesson learned: even in pop music, logos are serious business—especially when lawyers have too much free time.

11. Snowboarding into a $1 Million Mix-Up

Time for a "what would you do" scenario. Imagine waking up one day to find a company you worked with has mistakenly overpaid you $1 million in royalties. Now, imagine it's the same company you sued a few months ago for using your name without permission. What would you do? Would you return the money?

Olympic snowboarder Shaun White hasn't—at least not yet—when this exact scenario happened to him a few years ago.

Oakley, the well-known sunglasses brand, sued White after discovering they had accidentally overpaid him nearly $1 million in royalties. According to Oakley, the error occurred because they continued paying White for sales of their Holbrook eyewear even after their licensing agreement ended in December 2017.

At the same time, White had already taken Oakley to court, accusing the company of using his name and image to promote their products without his consent. This was particularly evident during the 2018 Winter Olympics, where his face appeared on posters and advertisements. White argued that Oakley had no right to use his likeness after their contract expired.

During a financial review, Oakley discovered the overpayment and demanded the money back. So far, White hasn't returned a cent. Now, the two sides are locked in a legal battle. Oakley wants their money back, while White claims the company owes him for exploiting his fame.

This ongoing legal drama has sparked a debate: Who's really at fault—Oakley for their accounting mistake or White for refusing to return the funds?

12. Barbie Goes to Court

What do you do when you're an artist with a message about society's treatment of women? If you're Tom Forsythe, you use Barbie dolls in provocative photos to make your point. Naturally, this bold move landed him in legal trouble—but it also sparked a powerful conversation.

In 1999, Forsythe, a Utah-based photographer, created "Food Chain Barbie," a series of photographs featuring nude Barbie dolls placed in domestic and sometimes unsettling scenarios. In one image titled "Malted Barbie," the doll was perched on a vintage malt machine in a provocative pose. Another shot, "Barbie Enchiladas," showed Barbies wrapped in tortillas, coated with salsa, and placed in an oven. Through these striking compositions, Forsythe critiqued how the Barbie brand objectifies women and reinforces outdated domestic ideals.

Mattel, the maker of Barbie, sued Forsythe for copyright infringement, calling his work offensive and a misrepresentation of their beloved doll. However, Forsythe argued that his art was a parody meant to spark reflection and not profit off Barbie's image.

The court sided with Forsythe. They ruled his work fell under "fair use," emphasizing its transformative, satirical nature. This 2003 ruling became a landmark decision in balancing artistic freedom with intellectual property rights.

13. The Strings Attached Lawsuit

In the world of guitars, even design inspirations can spark legal battles. This was the case when Gibson filed a trademark objection against PRS Guitars in 2023, accusing the company of borrowing design elements from Gibson's iconic and rare Theodore model. Originally introduced in 1957 as a prototype by Gibson's then-president Ted McCarty, the Theodore design gained a cult following despite its limited release. Fast-forward to modern times, PRS's new guitar model bore similarities to this classic, and Gibson wasn't happy.

Gibson claimed the PRS design infringed on Theodore's distinct aesthetic, such as its double-cutaway body with pointed horns. The objection became the latest episode in Gibson's ongoing quest to protect its legacy through legal action. However, PRS pushed back, stating their design was a unique creation, not a Theodore clone.

In an unexpected turn, PRS decided to drop the design altogether before the matter escalated further. The company maintained it wanted to focus on innovation rather than legal distractions. Gibson, meanwhile, celebrated the withdrawal as a victory in safeguarding its iconic designs.

This case highlights the fine line between honoring guitar heritage and protecting intellectual property.

14. A Software Showdown in Cyberspace

Imagine the internet back in the early '90s—just starting to bloom, modems buzzing, and websites looking like digital postcards. In the midst of this brave new digital world came CompuServe, Inc. v. Patterson, a case that paved the way for how the internet handles business disputes across state lines.

The story starts with Richard Patterson, a Texas resident who created a software program called "FlashPoint." He struck a deal with CompuServe, one of the OG internet service providers, to sell his software on their platform. Things were peachy until Patterson decided CompuServe wasn't playing fair with his intellectual property. So, he terminated the agreement. Or at least, he thought he did.

CompuServe fired back, filing a lawsuit in Ohio (where they were headquartered) for a declaratory judgment. Patterson, however, wasn't thrilled about being dragged into court hundreds of miles away. He argued Ohio had no jurisdiction over him—after all, he'd never stepped foot there! But the courts disagreed. Why? Because Patterson voluntarily did business with CompuServe, knowing they operated out of Ohio.

In the end, the court sided with CompuServe, setting a landmark precedent for online jurisdiction. The moral? If you're selling software online, don't be surprised if you're held accountable where your digital partners are based.

15. The One Where RIAA Sued a Family Without a Computer

In 2006, the RIAA (Recording Industry Association of America) filed lawsuits against 235 people, accusing them of illegally sharing music. One of the families they targeted? The Walls family is from Georgia—who didn't even own a computer.

When James Walls found out about the lawsuit, he was baffled. "How can they sue us when we don't even have a computer?" he asked. The RIAA's case relied on internet records that may have pointed to the wrong household. The Walls thought a previous homeowner or even identity theft could be to blame.

This wasn't the RIAA's only misstep. In another case, they sued a 15-year-old girl, Brittany Chan, after failing to prove a case against her mother. To pressure the family, the RIAA demanded they pay for a court-appointed legal guardian to represent Brittany. The cost? Thousands of dollars. The Chans stood their ground, and the judge eventually dismissed the case.

The RIAA's aggressive tactics, like suing innocent people and using shaky evidence, sparked outrage. Despite the backlash, the music industry giant didn't seem interested in changing its ways. For the Walls and the Chans, at least, the legal fight ended in small victories.

16. Microsoft vs. Eric Lam, Gordon Lam, and Melanie Suen (2009)

Microsoft's 2009 lawsuit took aim at a growing problem in the digital world: click fraud. This sneaky practice happens when people—or bots—click on online ads just to rack up charges or mess with data. It's like someone ringing your doorbell repeatedly and running away, but with serious financial consequences.

In this case, Microsoft accused several unnamed individuals of using shady tactics to inflate ad clicks. The goal? To harm advertisers and disrupt their campaigns. Click fraud chips away at the credibility of online advertising, leaving businesses wary.

Microsoft took the fight to court, determined to hold these fraudsters accountable. Their mission was clear: protect advertisers, secure their platform, and send a strong message to would-be scammers.

This lawsuit also shed light on a bigger issue. As digital ads grow, so do the risks. The case reminded everyone: online advertising needs to be fair. And sometimes, it takes a tech giant to call out the bad players and clean up the playground. Microsoft was ready to lead the charge.

17. From Scoops to Cease-and-Desists

Can you still like a company even if it sues you? For Nick Ciarelli, the answer was yes—despite Apple hitting him with a lawsuit for revealing their top-secret projects, much to their frustration.

Think Secret, the once-thriving Apple rumor website, met its end after a three-year legal battle with the tech giant. Apple sued Think Secret in 2005, accusing the site of publishing trade secrets and encouraging others to violate confidentiality agreements. The trouble started when the site leaked details about a mysterious, unreleased product codenamed "Asteroid."

The lawsuit quickly turned into a First Amendment debate, drawing support from digital rights groups like the Electronic Frontier Foundation. Think Secret stood its ground, continuing to publish insider scoops, including early looks at Mac OS X Leopard. Within the Apple rumor community, Apple's cease-and-desist letters became a sort of badge of honor—proof that a leak had hit the mark.

Eventually, the case was settled, and Think Secret shut down. Ciarelli never shared the terms of the settlement but stayed loyal to Apple, saying, "I didn't enjoy being sued, but I've always been a fan."

Apple may have won, but the saga serves as a cautionary tale for anyone daring to peek behind Cupertino's curtain.

Most Unusual Lawsuits From the Courtroom!

Who owns a selfie taken by a monkey? Can you sue God for terrorizing humanity? How about a man demanding a kidney back after his wife filed for divorce? These wild legal cases show that lawsuits can range from hilarious to thought-provoking. Some reveal the oddities of modern life, while others raise serious ethical questions.

1. The Elephant Lawsuit That Lasted a Decade

How far would you go to protect circus animals? Would you pay someone to back your case? That's what happened in a bitter legal battle between Feld Entertainment, owner of Ringling Brothers and Barnum & Bailey Circus, and the American Society for the Prevention of Cruelty to Animals (ASPCA).

It all started in 2000 when the ASPCA and other animal rights groups sued the circus, accusing it of mistreating elephants in violation of the Endangered Species Act. The case dragged on for nearly a decade. Then, in 2009, the court sided with Feld Entertainment. The judge found that the lawsuit relied on testimony from Tom Rider, a former circus employee, who was paid over $190,000 by the plaintiffs to support their claims.

Feld counter-sued and accused the ASPCA and others of racketeering. By 2012, the ASPCA agreed to settle and pay $9.3 million to end the fight. Feld's CEO, Kenneth Feld, called it a victory for their company and the people who care for their animals.

Food for thought: Would you have done the same as the ASPCA, or would you have played by the rules?

2. The Fight for Nonhuman Rights

What if a chimpanzee could go to court? That's the question the Nonhuman Rights Project (NhRP) brought to a New York courtroom in 2013. They filed a lawsuit on behalf of Tommy, a chimpanzee kept in private captivity. Their goal was ambitious: to have Tommy recognized as a legal "person" with the right to freedom.

The NhRP argued that chimpanzees, like humans, are self-aware, intelligent, and capable of complex emotions. Because of this, they deserve basic rights, including the right not to be held captive.

But the courts didn't see it that way. Judges ruled that chimpanzees aren't "legal persons" because they can't take on responsibilities or obligations. Appeals were filed, and new cases followed. Hercules and Leo, two chimps used in research, became the next plaintiffs. Once again, the courts denied their petitions.

Although the NhRP didn't win these battles, their lawsuits sparked something bigger: a global conversation about animal rights. The cases pushed the boundaries of how we view nonhuman animals and challenged us to consider what rights, if any, they should have.

3. The $650,000 Lawsuit Over Legacy

The worst thing about not having grandchildren from your son, who has been married for six years, is enduring the taunts of your friends and neighbors. Shame, shame, shame!

Sanjeev and Sadhana Prasad, aged 61 and 57, sued their son and daughter-in-law for failing to give them a grandchild after six years of marriage. Their demand was to either produce a grandchild within a year or pay back 50 million rupees ($650,000) for the emotional and financial toll they've endured.

"We had no choice but to take legal action," said Sadhana in an interview. "Every time we bring up the topic of grandchildren, they avoid the discussion. If they don't have children, our family name will end with them."

Sanjeev confirmed his wife's frustrations. "We're retired, and all we want is to be grandparents. Grandchildren bring joy and purpose to our lives, but we're being denied that happiness. We're even ready to take care of their kids."

While India's Supreme Court has acknowledged a son's obligation to care for his parents, campaigners argue that having children remains a personal choice, especially for women. Whose side are you on?

4. The Kidnapper Who Tried to Sue His Hostages

Imagine being a kidnapper who can't even trust his own hostages—what kind of world is that? That's exactly the question Jesse Dimmick seemed to be asking when he decided to sue Jared and Lindsay Rowley for breach of contract.

The whole bizarre saga started in September 2009 when Dimmick barged into the Rowleys' home near Topeka, claiming someone was out to kill him. Panicked and desperate, he struck a deal with the couple: if they hid him, he'd pay them an undisclosed sum of money.

The Rowleys played along. They fed Dimmick snacks and even watched Robin Williams' Patch Adams with him while sipping Dr Pepper and munching on Cheetos. When Dimmick eventually fell asleep, the couple made their escape unharmed.

Dimmick later filed his lawsuit in response to the Rowleys' $75,000 suit for emotional distress and trespassing. In handwritten court documents, he claimed the couple had violated their "legally binding oral contract" to hide him. He even demanded $235,000, partly to cover hospital bills after being shot by police during his arrest.

By May 2010, justice caught up with Dimmick. He was convicted of multiple felonies, including kidnapping, and sentenced to nearly 11 years in prison. Oh, and if that wasn't enough, he also had murder charges waiting for him in Colorado.

Needless to say, trust wasn't the only thing missing in this wild case.

5. When Hygiene Breaks a Marriage

There are plenty of reasons a marriage might fall apart: lack of love, compromise, or effort. But what about a lack of basic hygiene? That was the tipping point for a Turkish woman who sued her husband for divorce.

The woman told Ankara's 19th Family Court that her husband rarely showered, wore the same clothes for days, and brushed his teeth only once or twice a week. Witnesses, including coworkers and mutual acquaintances, testified to his poor hygiene. They described his smell as unbearable, with one coworker calling it "torturous" to work alongside him. Court documents revealed that the man would go 7-10 days without a shower, and his lack of dental care left him with terrible breath.

The court sided with the wife and granted her the divorce. As a parting gesture, the judge ordered the husband to pay her 500,000 Turkish lira (about $16,500) in compensation for enduring his hygiene habits. Sounds fair, wouldn't you agree?

6. From Yay to X-Ray

When a museum invites you to dive into fun, you don't expect to come out with an injury, right? But that's exactly what happened to Emily Robinson. She says she broke her ankle after jumping into the Museum of Ice Cream's Sprinkle Pool during a visit in 2022. Her injury was so bad that she needed surgery.

And she's not the only one. In August, another visitor, Jeremy Shorr, sued the museum after he also broke his ankle in the Sprinkle Pool. His injury was even worse—it needed surgery and metal implants. He blames the pool's design, saying the sprinkles were too shallow to cushion the landing.

People online have also shared their painful experiences. A TikTok video with three million views shows Carlie Noelle jumping off a mini diving board only to land hard on her tailbone in the sprinkles.

The lawsuits are still ongoing, and the Museum of Ice Cream is now under scrutiny for safety concerns. Will these cases lead to changes? That's still up in the air. But for now, the Sprinkle Pool is making headlines for all the wrong reasons.

7. An $8.8 Million Affair in North Carolina

Here's something surprising about North Carolina—it's one of the few states where you can sue someone for having an affair with your spouse before the marriage is officially over. That's exactly what *business owner Keith King did after learning that his wife had been in a 16-month relationship with a man named Francisco Huizar III. The court sided with King and ordered Huizar to pay a whopping $8.8 million in damages.*

Why so much? Most of it—$6.6 million—was meant to punish Huizar for his actions. The rest, $2.2 million, was to cover King's personal and business losses. According to his lawyer, the affair had a huge impact on both. King's wife, Danielle Swords, worked for his company, and after their split, the business suffered. Not only did he lose his wife, but he also lost an employee.

The lawsuit was built on several claims, including alienation of affection, emotional distress, and even assault and battery. It seems like in North Carolina, flings come with a million-dollar price tag.

8. The Case of Re A (Conjoined Twins)

The case of Re A (Conjoined Twins) is one of the most emotional and ethically challenging legal battles in modern medicine. It was about two conjoined twins, known as Jodie and Mary, who were born in Manchester, England. They were joined at the lower abdomen. Jodie was strong and healthy, but Mary was severely underdeveloped and completely dependent on Jodie to survive.

Doctors warned that without surgery, both twins would die within months. But separating them meant

Mary wouldn't survive—her body simply couldn't function on its own.

Their parents, who were devout Catholics, refused the surgery. They believed it wasn't their place to decide which child lived and which didn't. The hospital, however, took the case to court, arguing that Jodie had the right to life and that the surgery could save her.

The case went all the way to the Court of Appeal, which ruled in favor of the hospital. The judges decided that since Mary was entirely dependent on Jodie, the surgery wasn't an unlawful act but a way to save Jodie's life. The operation was carried out successfully, and Jodie survived.

The case remains a major turning point in medical ethics and legal history, raising tough questions about life, death, and difficult choices no family should ever have to make.

9. 69 Going on 49

People are often told they look or feel younger than they really are. But in 2018, Dutch motivational speaker Emile Ratelband took that idea to a whole new level—he went to court to legally change his age. At 69, he wanted his birth certificate to say he was born 20 years later. Why? Because he felt like he was in his 40s, both mentally and physically.

Ratelband claimed doctors told him his body was in great shape for his age. He argued this wasn't just about how he felt—it was about science backing him up. To make his case stronger, he compared his request to transgender rights. "If we can change our name or gender, why not our age?" he asked. He even offered to delay his pension for 20 years to prove he was serious.

While the court understood his argument, they pointed out that age is tied to laws, rights, and responsibilities. Changing it could cause all kinds of legal confusion. In the end, they ruled against him, saying age isn't as flexible as gender in legal terms.

Ratelband may not have won, but his case got people talking. It raised big questions about identity, personal freedom, and how much say we should have in defining ourselves.

10. Guardians of Cinema Etiquette

Imagine settling in to watch your favorite movie in 3-D, only for your date to spend the whole time glued to her phone. That's exactly what happened to Brandon Vezmar—and he was so annoyed that he sued her for $17.31, the price of her ticket to Guardians of the Galaxy Vol. 2.

According to Vezmar, his date started texting just minutes into the film. He claimed she checked her phone 10 to 20 times in the first 15 minutes, breaking the theater's no-texting rule and ruining the experience for him (and probably everyone around them).

It wasn't just about the money. Vezmar called her texting "a threat to civilized society" and later described the night as "a first date from hell."

The woman, who didn't want her name made public, said she was texting a friend who needed her. In the end, the lawsuit was dropped when she handed Vezmar $17.31 in cash—right in front of him. He even counted it.

This lawsuit makes you think: was it really about bad manners, or was his ego just bruised because she didn't love his favorite movie?

11. The Firefighter Who Feared Fire

Imagine being a teacher who's scared of kids or a lifeguard who's afraid of water. Sounds pretty funny, right? Well, meet Shayn Proler, a firefighter in Houston who was afraid of fire.

Proler was a captain in the Houston Fire Department who led a team in fire suppression. But things got messy when, in two separate incidents, the City of Houston claimed his fear of fire made him a liability. In 2004, another firefighter said Proler was too scared to enter a burning building. Then, in 2006, during a house fire, Proler reportedly couldn't put on his gear or follow orders. He even struggled to walk.

A doctor later diagnosed him with transient global amnesia, a temporary memory loss, but cleared him to go back to work. Even so, the city reassigned him to the training academy instead of active duty.

Feeling wronged, Proler filed a disability discrimination lawsuit. At first, a jury agreed and awarded him $362,000. However, the Texas Supreme Court stepped in and reversed that decision. They said fear of fire isn't a disability and pointed out that firefighting isn't exactly a "major life activity."

In the end, the court decided Proler wasn't disabled—just not cut out for firefighting. As they put it, "Reluctance to charge into a burning building is not a mental impairment; it's the normal human response."

What do you think? Should there be a fire in a firefighter's heart, or is it okay to be a little afraid of flames?

12. Who Really Owns a Monkey's Selfie?

You're a wildlife photographer. You leave your camera unattended. A monkey grabs it and takes a selfie. Who owns the copyright? According to PETA, the monkey does.

In 2011, a crested macaque named Naruto snapped a now-famous selfie using photographer David Slater's unattended camera. The photo went viral—and so did the legal battle. PETA stepped in, arguing that Naruto should own the rights to the "monkey selfie" and that any profits should go toward helping Naruto and other macaques.

Slater wasn't having it. He argued that while Naruto's timing was great, the picture wouldn't exist without his camera, setup, and planning. In 2016, a U.S. court ruled that animals can't hold copyrights. PETA appealed, but the 9th U.S. Circuit Court of Appeals upheld the decision, pointing out that PETA didn't even have a legal connection to Naruto in the first place.

Eventually, the case was settled out of court. Slater agreed to donate 25% of future earnings from the selfie to organizations protecting macaques in Indonesia. In the end, the law sided with humans—but Naruto's cheeky grin is still sparking debates about creativity, copyright, and whether animals should ever own their art.

13. The Plastic Surgery That Ended a Marriage

It all started as a charming love story. Feng, a man from northern China, met a stunning woman, married her, and they had a baby girl. The story took a surprising turn when Feng noticed something unusual about their newborn daughter. He thought she didn't look like either parent and, in his words, was "very unattractive." Suspicious, Feng accused his wife of infidelity. But she revealed a shocking secret—before their marriage, she had undergone extensive plastic surgery to transform her appearance.

Feeling betrayed, Feng filed a lawsuit against his wife, where he claimed she had deceived him by not disclosing her cosmetic surgeries. He argued this amounted to fraud. The case quickly gained attention and sparked heated debates around the world.

The court sided with Feng and ordered his wife to pay him $120,000 in damages because he had been misled into marrying her.

The lawsuit ignited discussions about trust in relationships and whether people should disclose past cosmetic procedures. It also raised bigger questions about society's obsession with beauty and the pressure to look a certain way.

14. The Dexter Ad That Led to a Scare

Michael C. Hall has an intense look, which made him perfect for Dexter. But could his face actually scare someone so much that they sue?

In 2019, a New York woman, Anjanaffy Njewadda, took Showtime Networks to court, claiming a subway ad for Dexter caused her to panic. The ad featured Hall's face wrapped in plastic, which gave off a seriously creepy vibe.

Njewadda said the image was so disturbing that she panicked, lost her footing on the subway stairs, and injured her foot and ankle. She blamed Showtime, CBS, the MTA, and the New York City Transit Authority, arguing they were negligent for putting such a terrifying ad in a public space.

The companies argued that her reaction wasn't something they could have predicted, so they weren't responsible. The court agreed. The judge ruled that the ad wasn't extreme enough to create liability and dismissed the case.

Njewadda didn't win her lawsuit, but one thing's for sure—Dexter left more than just a psychological mark on New York subway riders.

15. Lost in the Fantasy of Beer Ads

Did you know that cracking open a cold Bud Light would transport you to a tropical paradise, where crystal-clear beaches, endless fun, and attractive people await? No? That's because it won't—it's just an ad. In 1991, Richard Overton learned the hard way when he filed a lawsuit against Anheuser-Busch, claiming their commercials were misleading. He argued the ads made people believe Bud Light could turn their lives into a vacation-worthy fantasy.

Overton's dreams of paradise were dashed, and so were his legal claims. The Michigan Court of Appeals ruled the ads were simply "puffery," a fancy legal term for harmless exaggerations. The court explained that no reasonable person would actually expect a beer to come with a ticket to paradise.

In the end, Overton's case went flat, leaving the courts to remind us all that while a Bud Light might deliver good vibes, it won't deliver a beach vacation.

16. A Man's Fight to Be Recognized for Himself

There's nothing quite like being recognized for who you truly are, flaws and all. But for Allen Heckard, that wasn't possible. In 2006, he filed a lawsuit against NBA icon Michael Jordan and Nike, claiming he was fed up with constant comparisons to the basketball legend.

Heckard's only wish was to be acknowledged as himself, just like Jordan is known for being Jordan. In fact, Heckard argued that since he was older, it was actually Jordan who resembled him. The similarities, however, made his life stressful and exhausting.

Whether at church or playing basketball at the park, people constantly stopped him to comment on how much he looked like Jordan. "I can't go anywhere without being harassed," Heckard said in an interview. "I should be able to live my life, but people always think I'm him."

Heckard represented himself in court and claimed this issue had followed him for 15 years. He filed the lawsuit in Oregon, seeking $416 million from both Jordan and Nike CEO Phil Knight. Why Nike? Because Nike made Jordan a global star and contributed to his struggles.

Ultimately, Heckard dropped the case later that year. Maybe he realized that looking like a legend isn't the worst problem to have.

17. Robert Brock's $5 Million Lawsuit Against... Robert Brock

Is life in prison so illuminating it sparks genius ideas? For Robert Lee Brock, it seems so. The inmate, serving 23 years for breaking and entering and grand larceny, decided to file a $5 million lawsuit—against himself. Why? Because he believed he had violated his own civil rights by getting arrested. Oh, and naturally, he asked the state to pay up because, well, he couldn't afford it from behind bars.

In a seven-page, handwritten masterpiece submitted to federal court, Brock argued that in 1993, he drank alcohol, which went against his religious beliefs. This poor decision, according to Brock, led to his arrest and, thus, a violation of his civil rights. "I want to pay myself $5 million," he declared. "But since I'm a ward of the state and can't earn money, I'm asking the state to pay it on my behalf."

The judge wasn't sold on Brock's groundbreaking legal theory. "While this is an innovative approach to civil rights litigation," she noted, "the claim—and the requested relief—are utterly ridiculous." The case was promptly dismissed as frivolous.

Brock's creative attempt to mess around with the system may not have earned him millions, but it certainly earned some laughs.

18. That Time When Uber Ruined a Marriage

A man in France took Uber to court for $48 million because it ruined his marriage. What happened? No, he wasn't an employee fired by Uber. No, he didn't get into a fight during a ride. Uber accidentally revealed his whereabouts to his wife.

According to the man, he had borrowed his wife's iPhone and logged into the Uber app. Even after logging out, the app continued to send notifications about his rides to her phone. It seems those notifications didn't align with what his wife wanted to see, as the marriage ended soon after.

He demanded Uber fork over $48 million as payment for his marital troubles. Interestingly, the glitch reportedly only affected iPhones and didn't occur on Android devices.

The lawsuit brought attention to the potential consequences of tech glitches on personal lives, but the outcome remains a mystery. Whether or not he won the case, it's clear this is one of the more unusual examples of app-related lawsuits.

19. The Mom Who Dared to Parent

Ah, teenagers and their phones! In Spain, a 15-year-old boy was so angry when his mother confiscated his phone that he took her to court. He claimed her actions were mistreatment because she took away his beloved device to encourage him to focus on his studies. The horror of losing access to your phone to perform better at school! He even demanded that his mother face jail time and cover his legal costs.

The peculiar case made its way to a judge in Almeria, located in southern Spain. Ultimately, the judge sided with the mom, ruling that she had every right to take the phone and acted responsibly. The court declared that her actions were in her son's best interest and necessary for his education.

"She wouldn't be a responsible mother if she let her son get distracted by his phone and neglect his studies," the court stated in its decision. Parents worldwide take note—you might have the law on your side when enforcing screen time limits!

20. The Big Desk Bang

Hearing loss can come from many sources—concerts, headphones, fireworks, or even firearms. But who would've thought a loud slap on a desk could cause such harm? A 16-year-old high school student in Connecticut claimed that his math teacher caused significant hearing damage when she smacked her hand on his desk to wake him up during class. The student, Vinicios Robacher, and his family took legal action against the school, the school board, and the city.

According to his father, Soel Robacher, the boy's left ear was pressed against the desk when the teacher's loud bang ruptured his eardrum. The incident allegedly left Vinicios with severe hearing loss. Though some of his hearing has since returned, he's undergone multiple treatments and may still require surgery to repair the damage fully.

Despite the allegations, the case ultimately went nowhere. It's safe to say this lawsuit didn't make much noise in court.

21. Betrayed, Divorced, and Down a Kidney

How much do you love your spouse? Enough to donate a kidney? But what happens when love turns sour? Dr. Richard Batista from Long Island sued his ex-wife, Dawnell Batista, demanding the return of the kidney he had donated to her during their marriage—or $1.5 million in compensation.

The couple's relationship started like a fairytale. They met while he was a surgeon, and she was training to be a nurse. In 2001, Richard donated his kidney to save Dawnell's life. But things took a dark turn. Dawnell filed for divorce in 2005, and Richard alleged she'd been having an affair not long after receiving the transplant. On top of the heartbreak, Richard claimed he was denied contact with their three children for extended periods.

Richard voiced his demands publicly, but the court ultimately decided his fate. Relying on the legal principle that human organs cannot be treated as property in a divorce, his request was rejected. While Richard lost both the case and his kidney, he stood by his choice to save her life, even if it came with the pain of a broken heart.

22. Gerald Mayo vs. The Devil and His Minions

Did you know you can't sue a nonphysical entity? It's not because they don't exist (debatable), but because there's no address to deliver legal papers. That's exactly why one bizarre lawsuit was thrown out in 1971.

Gerald Mayo, a 22-year-old inmate, was deeply dissatisfied with the direction his life had taken. Locked away during what he believed should have been his prime years, he began searching for someone to blame. After some reflection, Mayo reached an unusual conclusion: Satan was the root of his troubles. He soon filed a lawsuit against the devil and his minions.

Mayo claimed that Satan had deliberately caused him misery, created obstacles in his life, and led him to ruin. He sought legal retribution for what he described as deliberate wickedness against him. However, the case hit an obstacle. Without an earthly address for Satan, the court couldn't serve him with legal papers. The judge ruled that the metaphysical defendant couldn't be held accountable, and the case was dismissed.

23. The Devilish W-2 Tax Form

If you think the devil only makes appearances in religious texts, think again. He also appears in W-2 tax forms! In Tennessee, a man quit his job because his W-2 tax form had the number "666" on it. Walter Slonopas, a 52-year-old born-again Christian, believed the number was the mark of the devil. For him, faith mattered more than a paycheck, so he took legal action against his employer.

This wasn't Walter's first encounter with the dreaded digits. When he started at Revstone Corp. in 2011, he was accidentally assigned "666" as his clock-in number. After raising the issue, it was changed to 668. But a few months later, during a system update, the ominous number came back. He quit again, protesting what he saw as a bad omen, but eventually returned after receiving yet another new number.

The final straw came with the infamous W-2 form. Slonopas called it "unbelievable" and refused to file his taxes until the company issued a different form. A company executive clarified that the number simply reflected the order in which documents were mailed, but Walter wasn't buying it.

You have to wonder… does Walter check his grocery receipts for 666, too?

24. The Bubble Prank That Floated Into Court

Why would anyone sue over bubbles? They're light, fun, and harmless—until you slip. In the early hours of July 7, 2001, a prankster poured gallons of Joy dish soap into a public fountain located in Duluth, Minnesota. The result? An eight-foot mountain of bubbles.

Attracted by the soapy spectacle, 57-year-old Kathy Kelly couldn't resist walking into the frothy mess. Unfortunately, she slipped, fell, and cut her leg. For Kelly, a diabetic, this wasn't a minor injury. The wound became gangrenous, which led to $43,000 in medical bills.

Kelly sued the city because it hadn't acted quickly enough to clean up the fountain or warn the public. A St. Louis County jury agreed, holding Duluth 70% responsible for her injuries. They awarded her $125,000 in damages and concluded that taxpayers should foot the bill for not addressing the bubble-filled fountain promptly.

The jury did assign Kelly 30% of the blame for her decision to wade into the suds, but the prankster escaped any legal responsibility. One juror even argued taxpayers should have been held 90% liable. On the bright side, at least no one tried to sue the soap manufacturer!

25. A College Promise That Fell Short

It seemed like a simple plan: go to college, graduate, and get a job. But for Trina Thompson, things didn't work out that way. The 27-year-old Monroe College graduate from New York sued her school, saying they hadn't helped her find a job.

Thompson earned a degree in information technology. After graduation, she struggled to get hired. She blamed the college's career counselors, saying they *hadn't done what they promised. She wanted a $70,000 tuition refund because the school hadn't given her the job support they had advertised.*

In her lawsuit, Thompson said she had reached out to companies listed on Monroe's website. Only two had responded, and neither had hired her. She believed the school's career center had focused on students with perfect 4.0 GPAs. With her 2.7 GPA, she felt she had been ignored, even though she had worked hard and had good attendance.

Thompson said she had done her part, but the college had failed her. Her case made people question: Do schools really owe students a job after graduation?

26. The Bar That Served Too Much or the Driver Who Had Too Many?

A South Carolina woman sued a bar after a car accident left her paralyzed. In 2009, 22-year-old Chelsea Hess crashed her car after leaving Jock's Sports Grill in Beaufort, South Carolina. The accident caused a severe spinal cord injury, which left her unable to walk.

Hess blamed the bar for serving her too much alcohol. She said they kept giving her drinks even though she was clearly drunk. In her lawsuit, she argued that the bar should have stopped serving her and made sure she didn't drive. She claimed Jock's Sports Grill broke South Carolina's liquor laws, which say businesses can't serve alcohol to people who are already too intoxicated.

Hess asked for money to cover her medical bills, lost wages, and the lifelong impact of her injury. But the court dismissed the case, ruling that Hess was responsible for her own choices.

The case sparked debate. Should bars be held accountable for drunk drivers, or is it always the driver's responsibility? While Hess didn't win, her lawsuit brought attention to the risks of alcohol over-service and drunk driving. It also raised tough questions about blame, responsibility, and the role of businesses in keeping people safe.

27. Don't Be Too Kind With Your Neighbours

No good deed goes unpunished, or so it seemed, for two Colorado teens in 2004. Taylor Ostergaard, 18, and Lindsey Zellitti, 19, decided to skip a dance and spend their evening baking cookies. Their plan was to deliver the treats anonymously to neighbors in their rural Durango community. Each plate came with a heart-shaped card signed by "The T and L Club."

But their good intentions took a wrong turn at Wanita Renea Young's door. When the teens knocked around 10:30 p.m., the 49-year-old panicked. She'd been burglarized before and feared trouble was at her doorstep. Young called the police, and although no crime had been committed, the ordeal caused her such anxiety that she ended up in the hospital.

Young later sued the teens for $900 to cover her medical expenses, claiming their late-night visit caused her distress. A court ended up ruling in her favor.

The case sparked debates about whether acts of kindness should ever come with a price. Despite the setback, the teens vowed to keep spreading goodwill, no matter the cost.

28. Suing God for Justice

In 2008, Nebraska State Senator Ernie Chambers filed a lawsuit that got attention around the world. Who was he suing? God. Chambers asked the court for a permanent order against the Almighty, accusing Him of causing "widespread death, destruction, and terror." He claimed these acts were like threats against him and his community.

Chambers said the lawsuit wasn't a joke. He wanted to show that courts should be open to everyone, rich or poor. But there was one big problem: God doesn't have an address. Because of that, the judge dismissed the case, saying it was impossible to serve legal papers to God.

Chambers didn't give up easily. He argued that since the court acknowledged God's existence, His omniscience should count as notice of the lawsuit. Still, the case didn't go any further.

Even though the lawsuit was dismissed, it sparked debates about the justice system, divine accountability, and creative ways to make a point.

29. Lady Gaga's Dognapping Drama

Lady Gaga's real life could inspire a movie—a dognapping drama.

In 2021, two of Lady Gaga's French bulldogs, Koji and Gustav, were stolen in a violent robbery. Her dog walker, Ryan Fischer, was shot in the chest and rushed to the hospital. Gaga offered a $500,000 reward, saying she just wanted her dogs back—no questions asked.

Two days later, Jennifer McBride returned the dogs, claiming she found them and wanted to keep them safe. But soon, police discovered she had ties to the thieves. She later pleaded no contest to receiving stolen property and was sentenced to two years of probation.

In 2023, McBride took things even further—she sued Gaga. She not only demanded the $500,000 reward but also asked for an extra $1.5 million in damages. She accused Gaga of fraud and breach of contract. Gaga's legal team fought back, arguing that McBride couldn't profit from her own crime. The court agreed, ruling that she had "unclean hands."

In the end, the judge sided with Gaga. McBride walked away with nothing—except a legal lesson that crime really doesn't pay.

Classic Lawsuits - How History Was Written!

From cannibalism and runaway coachmen to decomposed snails and drowned sheep, history is packed with lawsuits that shaped the laws we still follow today.

These cases set important legal precedents that still impact how courts handle negligence, property rights, contract law, and even personal injury claims. Some were groundbreaking, others were downright ridiculous, but all of them played a role in shaping legal history.

1. The Butcher, the Coachman, and a Broken Leg (1789)

Have you ever wondered about the early cases that shaped personal injury law? Here's one that set an important precedent.

In 1789, a London butcher named George Ormond had an unfortunate run-in—literally—with a royal carriage. The collision left him with a broken leg, and he decided to take legal action. But instead of suing the coachman who caused the accident, Ormond went after Don Payne, the estate manager of the Prince of Wales's residence, Carlton House. Payne was legally responsible for the coachman's actions.

According to Ormond, the crash was reckless driving. He claimed the coachman, George Smith, was in a hurry and had been drinking. Ormond testified that as soon as the horses were harnessed, Smith climbed into the driver's seat, downed a glass of gin, whipped the horses, and sped off. The jury believed Ormond's account and ruled in his favor. Payne was found liable, and Ormond was awarded £100 in damages—roughly £13,900 in today's money.

The Ormond v Payne case helped establish a key legal principle—employers can be held responsible for the negligent actions of their employees. It's a rule that still plays a major role in personal injury law today.

2. The Smoke Ball That Rewrote Contract Law (1892)

Back in the late 1800s, miracle cures were all the rage. The Carbolic Smoke Ball Company jumped on the trend with a quirky flu remedy—a rubber ball filled with carbolic acid vapor that users inhaled through their noses. They made a bold promise: if you used the smoke ball as directed but still caught the flu, they'd pay you £100 (about £11,500 in today's money). To show they were serious, they even deposited £1,000 in the bank.

This is where things got more interesting. During the 1892 flu epidemic, Elizabeth Carlill, a writer and lawyer's wife, bought the product, used it as instructed, and still got sick. The company refused to pay when she tried to claim her £100. So, Carlill took them to court. The judge ruled in her favor, stating the ad was a genuine offer and Carlill had met the conditions. She won her £100.

Ironically, Carlill lived to 96—only to die of influenza decades later.

The Carlill v Carbolic Smoke Ball Co case became a game-changer in contract law. It proved that advertisements could be legally binding if they made clear promises with specific conditions. Today, it's one of the most famous contract law cases in history.

3. The Flick Knife That Sparked a Legal Debate (1960)

In 1959, a new law made it illegal to sell certain weapons, including flick knives. But could simply displaying one in a shop window land you in trouble? That's what happened to James Bell, a Bristol shopkeeper who put a flick knife on display with a price tag of four shillings. A police inspector saw it and accused him of breaking the law.

Bell ended up in court, but the case was thrown out. Why? Because under contract law, putting something in a shop window isn't technically an "offer" to sell—it's just an "invitation to treat." In simpler terms, it's like saying, "Hey, this is available!" rather than, "I am legally promising to sell this to you." The actual "offer" happens when a customer brings money to the counter. Since the law only banned "offering" weapons for sale—and not "offering or exposing" them—Bell hadn't broken any rules.

The Fisher v Bell case became a perfect example of how contract law and criminal law sometimes clash. The court had to stick to the legal definition of "offer," even though the whole point of the law was to prevent the sale of dangerous weapons. Bell walked free, and the case became a classic in legal textbooks.

4. The Snail That Shaped Modern Law (1932)

One of Britain's weirdest legal battles started with a rotten snail and a bottle of ginger beer. In August 1928, May Donoghue went to a café in Paisley and enjoyed a drink her friend had bought for her. But as she sipped, she made a horrifying discovery—the decomposed remains of a snail floating inside. She fell seriously ill and wanted to take legal action. There was just one problem: since she hadn't bought the drink herself, she couldn't sue for breach of contract.

So, Donoghue went after the manufacturer instead, arguing they had a duty to keep their drinks snail-free. The case made its way to Lord Atkin, who introduced the now-famous "neighbor principle." His ruling stated that people must take reasonable care to avoid actions that could harm their "neighbors"—not just the people next to them, but anyone directly affected by what they do (or don't do).

Donoghue was awarded £200 (about £12,500 today), but her case left a much bigger impact. The Donoghue v Stevenson case made it possible for people to sue when companies fail to keep them safe. Some praise it as a milestone for consumer rights—others blame it for fueling today's compensation culture.

5. How Two Neighbors Shaped Nuisance Law (1879)

Ever had a noisy neighbor drive you up the wall? That's exactly what happened in this case, except it wasn't loud music or a barking dog—it was a candy maker pounding away in his kitchen.

Dr. Octavius Sturges, a London physician, lived next door to Mr. Bridgman, a confectioner who had been using giant mortar and pestles for his business for 20 years. No one had ever complained. But when Dr. Sturges built a consulting room at the end of his garden—right up against Bridgman's kitchen—the noise became unbearable.

The doctor took Bridgman to court, demanding that he stop. Bridgman argued he'd been making candy this way for two decades, so he had every right to continue. The court disagreed. It ruled that just because no one complained before didn't mean it wasn't a nuisance now. Since the noise only became a problem after the consulting room was built, the confectioner's history didn't protect him.

The Sturges v Bridgman case set two big legal precedents. First, whether something is a nuisance depends on its surroundings—what's intolerable in a quiet neighborhood might be fine in an industrial area. Second, a nuisance claim needs to be ongoing for the full 20 years to be protected by long-term use.

6. The Policeman's Foot and the Law That Followed (1968)

Imagine accidentally running over someone's foot—then deciding to just leave the car there. That's exactly what happened in 1968 when Vincent Fagan found himself in a bizarre legal battle after driving onto the foot of police officer David Morris in north London.

At first, it was an accident. But when the officer told him to move the car, Fagan refused and let the poor officer stand there in pain. That decision landed him in court, charged with "assaulting a constable in the execution of his duties." He was convicted but appealed, arguing that because the initial act was unintentional, it couldn't be considered an assault.

The court ruled that while driving onto the officer's foot wasn't intentional, refusing to move the car showed intent. This decision led to what's now called the "doctrine of the continuing act."

The Fagan v Metropolitan Police Commissioner case became a big deal in criminal law. It established that if an act is still happening, intent (mens rea) can develop later, making someone legally responsible. The exception? Strict liability crimes like speeding, where intent doesn't matter—you're guilty whether you meant to do it or not.

7. A Shipwreck Case That Washed Away in Court (1874)

Losing livestock at sea is bad enough, but losing a legal battle over it adds insult to injury. In this historic case, a ship owner was transporting sheep to Great Britain when a storm hit, sending several animals overboard. The sheep's owner, understandably upset, took legal action and claimed the ship owner had violated the Contagious Diseases (Animals) Act 1869.

This law required animals to be transported in pens to prevent the spread of disease. The plaintiff argued that if the sheep had been properly penned, they wouldn't have been lost. But the court saw things differently. While the ship owner had technically broken the law, the judges ruled that the Act was intended to control disease, not to protect animals from being washed away. Since the harm suffered wasn't the type the law was meant to prevent, the case was thrown out.

The Gorris v Smith lawsuit clarified an important legal principle: if a statute is designed to prevent one type of harm, it can't be stretched to cover something else, even if the end result seems unfair.

8. Murder on the High Seas (1884)

Some legal cases make history, and some push the boundaries of law and morality—this one did both. In 1884, four sailors—Tom Dudley, Edwin Stephens, Edmund Brooks, and Richard Parker—found themselves stranded in the middle of the ocean after a storm wrecked their yacht. With no food, no water, and no rescue in sight, desperation took hold.

After 19 days adrift, Dudley and Stephens made a grim decision: they would kill and eat Parker, the youngest and weakest among them, to stay alive. Brooks refused to take part, but the other two went through with it. Four days later, a passing ship rescued them, and soon after, they were charged with murder in England.

At trial, Dudley and Stephens argued that they had no choice. The court ruled that necessity is no excuse for murder, no matter how dire the situation. Both men were found guilty but later received a royal pardon. Their sentence was reduced to six months in prison.

The R v Dudley and Stephens case set a lasting precedent in criminal law: survival isn't a legal defense for taking an innocent life. It also sparked fierce debates about morality, law, and just how far humans will go to stay alive.

9. The Fox Farm vs The Spiteful Neighbor (1936)

Some legal battles start with contracts, theft, or injuries. This one started with foxes and gunfire. The 1936 case of Hollywood Silver Fox Farm v Emmett is a classic example of how being a bad neighbor can land you in court.

Hollywood Silver Fox Farm bred silver foxes for their valuable fur. But these foxes were extremely sensitive to noise. A loud sound could send them into a panic, harming their breeding or even causing vixens to kill their own cubs.

Mr. Emmett was a neighboring farmer with a grudge against the fox farm. Instead of settling things peacefully, he chose revenge. He started firing shotguns near the fox pens, knowing the noise would terrify the animals and disrupt the business. He wasn't hunting or protecting his land—he was just being spiteful.

The court ruled in favor of the fox farm and called Emmett's actions a private nuisance. The key lesson? Even if something is technically legal, if you do it just to harm someone else, the law might not be on your side.

10. The Apprentice Who Fought for His Jewel (1722)

Some legal cases are complex, but Armory v Delamirie (1722) was as simple as "finders keepers."

A young chimney sweep's apprentice found a valuable jewel while cleaning. Curious about its worth, he took it to a goldsmith named Mr. Delamirie. But instead of being honest, Delamirie saw an opportunity. He took the jewel out of its setting and offered the boy a small sum. When the boy refused and asked for his jewel back, Delamirie returned only the empty setting—the jewel was gone.

Feeling cheated, the apprentice went to court. The judge ruled in his favor, saying that someone who finds a lost item has a legal right to keep it—unless the original owner comes forward. As punishment for keeping the jewel, Delamirie had to compensate the boy based on the highest possible value of the missing gem.

This case became a major lesson in property law. It showed that even finders have rights, and trying to cheat them can backfire. Armory v Delamirie is still cited today, proving that greed can cost you more than just what you tried to take.

Afterword

We hope you enjoyed these wild lawsuit stories of corporate clashes, innocent men and women taking on the world, and the craziest lawsuits going back to even the 1700's and 1800's.

Which story did you enjoy the most? Which ones are you most keen to share with your school, work friends, or family?

If you have any issues with the content inside, please email us at benmaddison.9hf2t@simplelogin.com.

If you LOVED the book, please help our small publishing company out by leaving a kind review on Amazon, or wherever you purchased the book!

Thank you for reading!

Yours, Thomas Maddison.

About the Author

Thomas Maddison is an emerging author of law-related publications. This is Thomas's debut book.

Bibliography

Bringhurst, Robert. The Elements of Typographic Style. Version 3.2. Point Roberts: Hartley & Marks, 2004.

The Chicago Manual of Style. 17th ed. The University of Chicago Press Editorial Staff. Chicago: The University of Chicago Press, 2017. https://www.chicagomanualofstyle.org/.

Vellum Tutorial. Updated regularly. Oakland and Seattle: 180g. https://help.vellum.pub/tutorial/.

Printed in Dunstable, United Kingdom

75408765R00061